Chess for Kids

*A Foundational Guide for Bringing
Chess Masters out of Children*

Table of Contents

Introduction

Chess has been played for centuries. It is a game of strategy, patience, and skill and is enjoyed by people of all ages. Many parents and educators recognize the benefits of teaching children how to play chess. It can help children develop critical thinking skills, improve concentration, and boost self-confidence. It is also a great way to introduce children to the world of competitive sports and teach them the value of perseverance and practice.

"Chess for Kids: A Foundational Guide for Bringing Chess Masters Out of Children" is a comprehensive guide that will teach you the basics of chess and help them develop into skilled players. This book is designed to be an accessible and easy-to-understand resource that parents, teachers, and children can use together to learn the game of chess.

The book begins with an introduction to the history of chess and the various pieces used in the game. It then moves on to the rules of the game and the basic strategies involved in playing chess.

Consider this the start of a thrilling journey into the world of chess. With enough time and patience, you will discover why this game is even more popular than ever.

Chapter 1: The Game of Chess

Chess isn't new. It is a very, very old game that has been around for hundreds of years. Imagine that! It's a treasure from the past that's still being explored and enjoyed today.

Chess is believed to have originated in Northern India around 1500 years ago. Back then, it was called "chaturanga," which means "four divisions of the military:" infantry, cavalry, elephants, and chariots. These were represented by the pieces pawn, knight, bishop, and rook, respectively.

Over the years, chess has traveled far and wide, changed and evolved, and has become the game everyone knows and loves today.

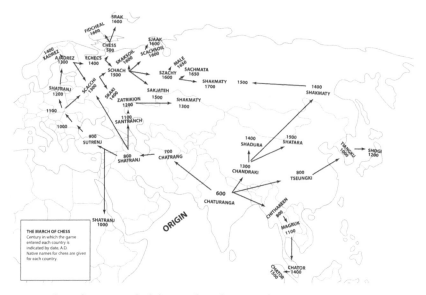

1. *Chess has traveled far and wide over the centuries. Source: https://www.vividmaps.com/wp-content/uploads/2017/06/Chess.jpg*

Now, you might be wondering why so many around the world love to play chess. Well, there are many reasons!

First, chess is basically a beautiful puzzle that never gets old. Each game is different, and there's always something new to learn. It's a game that challenges your intellect and concentration skills.

Second, anyone can play chess: young or old, boy or girl, beginner or expert. It doesn't matter who you are or where you come from; the chessboard is for everybody.

Finally, in chess, all that matters are your moves and your strategies.

Now, let's talk about the chessboard itself. A chessboard is a battlefield on which your pieces fight. It's a square board divided into 64 smaller squares. Half of the squares are black, and the other half are white, in a checkerboard pattern.

The chessboard is set up in a way that a white square is always in the right-hand corner. Each player will have 16 pieces: one king, one queen, two rooks, two knights, two bishops, and eight pawns. Don't worry if you don't know what these pieces do yet, we'll get to that soon!

Remember, the board is your playground, and the pieces are your team. And just like a great team captain, your job is to guide your team to victory!

The Aim of Playing Chess

Now that you've gotten a glimpse of where chess comes from and why it's so popular let's talk about the game's main goal.

In chess, your number one mission is to protect your king while trying to capture that of your opponent.

When you put your opponent's king in a position where it can be captured (this is called a checkmate), you win the game! But remember, your opponent will also be trying to do the same. So, you will have to keep both offense and defense in mind.

Chess is a workout for your brain! It helps you think better and faster and improves your problem-solving skills.

When you're playing chess, you have to plan ahead, analyze the situation on the board, and make decisions that will benefit you in the game. You're a detective trying to figure out your opponent's plans and coming up with strategies to outsmart them. Over time, you'll notice that you're getting better at chess and becoming a sharper thinker in general!

2. *Chess requires a lot of planning and analysis. Source:
https://unsplash.com/photos/nAjil1z3eLk?utm_source=unsplash&
utm_medium=referral&utm_content=creditShareLink*

Chess is not just about winning or losing. It's also about learning valuable life skills that will help you in the real world. Let's talk about a few of them.

Firstly, chess teaches you patience. Rushing your moves can lead to mistakes, and these mistakes can cost you the game. Just like in life, good things often take time. Chess helps you understand this and teaches you to be patient.

Secondly, it's all about strategy. It's not enough to just know how the pieces move; you need to have a plan. You need to think about your current moves and how they will affect the game. This strategic thinking can come in handy in everyday life too!

Finally, chess develops foresight. You always need to be a few steps ahead, anticipating your opponent's moves and planning your response. This ability to look ahead and prepare for what's coming is a valuable life skill.

Chess is so much more than just a game. It's a fun, challenging adventure that can help you become smarter and even teaches you important life skills.

The Nature of Chess

You know how some games are all about luck, where you have to cross your fingers and hope for the best? Well, chess isn't one of those games. Chess is a game of strategy and planning. You're a general in a grand battle, planning your moves, setting up traps, and launching attacks.

Every move you make on the board should be part of a bigger plan. Sometimes, you'll have to attack your opponent's pieces. Other times, you'll have to defend your own pieces. And sometimes, you'll want to do something sneaky, like setting up a trap for an unsuspecting piece. All these tactics make chess an intense and thrilling game.

During a game of chess, it's just you and your opponent, each with an army of 16 pieces. You and your opponent take turns making moves. This means you'll have time to think about your move when it's your opponent's turn. But it also means you have to be patient and wait for your turn to come around again.

And just as in life, fairness is key. Each player starts with the same pieces, the same opportunities, and the same chance to win. How you use your pieces and your opportunities will determine the outcome of the game.

Remember, chess is not just about winning. It's about playing fair, respecting your opponent, and enjoying the journey.

Why Learn Chess?

Chess is basically a workout for your brain. It's an amazing game with many benefits, especially for children like you. Let's discover some of these benefits together.

Cognitive Development

When you play chess, you give your brain a good workout. Just like exercising strengthens your muscles, playing chess makes you smarter.

It can improve your memory because you always have to remember how the different pieces move and recall previous games you've played. It can also boost your creativity as you think of new strategies and unexpected moves to surprise your opponent. Plus, it can improve your thinking as you analyze the situation on the chessboard.

So, playing chess regularly can help you become a smarter, quicker, and more creative thinker.

Problem-Solving Skills

Every game of chess is a new puzzle waiting to be solved. You and your opponent are always making moves and counter-moves, creating problems for each other to solve.

Maybe your opponent is threatening one of your pieces, or maybe you're stuck in a difficult position. What do you do? You have to think, analyze the situation, and find a solution. These problem-solving skills are not just useful on the chessboard. They're also very helpful in real life. Whether it's a tricky math problem or a challenging situation at school, being a good problem solver can help you a lot.

Concentration

Have you ever tried to do something really difficult while loud music was playing or people were talking around you? It's hard, right? That's because difficult tasks require concentration. And guess what? Chess can improve your concentration.

When you're playing chess, you need to focus on the game. You can't be distracted by what's happening around you. You have to pay attention to the chessboard, remember your plan, think about your next move, and keep an eye on what your opponent is doing.

The more you play chess, the better you'll become at concentrating. And just like problem-solving skills, good concentration can help you in many areas of your life, from doing your homework to playing sports.

The Thrill of the Game

Some people might think chess is boring because there's no running around or jumping like in physical sports. But they couldn't be more wrong! Chess is full of excitement, suspense, and fun. Let's explore some of the reasons why it is such a thrilling game.

The Battle of Minds

When you play chess, you go head to head against another person in a thrilling battle of minds. You and your opponent, the main characters in an exciting adventure, each try to outwit the other.

Every move your opponent makes is a new mystery. What are they planning? How can you respond? There's a lot of excitement in trying to figure out your opponent's strategy and planning your counterattack.

The Joy of Strategy

One of the most exciting parts of chess is coming up with your own strategies and tactics. You have to plan your moves, launch attacks, defend your pieces, and set traps for your opponent.

There's a great sense of satisfaction when a strategy works out as you planned. And even when it doesn't, there's always the excitement of learning, adjusting your strategy, and doing better in the next game.

The Surprise Element

Chess is full of surprises. Just when you think you're winning, your opponent might make an unexpected move that changes the whole game. You might even find a brilliant move that turns the tables in your favor.

These twists and turns keep the game exciting and unpredictable. They teach you to be flexible and adaptable, always ready to respond to new challenges.

The Race to Checkmate

The ultimate goal of chess is to put your opponent's king in checkmate. Nothing beats the rush you get as you're close to making a checkmate.

But remember, the journey to checkmate is just as exciting as the move itself. Every move you make, every piece you capture, every strategy you employ adds to the thrill of the game.

Key Takeaways

- Chess originated in India over 1500 years ago and has spread worldwide over the centuries.

- It provides mental stimulation and challenges players to think strategically. It helps develop problem-solving, concentration, and logical thinking skills.

- The objective of chess is to capture the opponent's king by putting it in checkmate. Players take turns making moves, and the game requires both attack and defense strategies.

- Luck has no place in chess. Success depends on planning, strategizing, anticipating the opponent's moves, and making good decisions.

- It teaches valuable life skills like patience, strategic thinking, and foresight.

- Playing chess exercises the brain and improves cognitive functions like memory and creativity. It also boosts concentration.

- It provides an intellectual challenge and thrill as two minds battle each other through strategizing and making surprising moves. Players try to figure out each other's strategies to gain an advantage.

Chapter 2: Meet the Characters; Chess Pieces and Their Moves

Each piece on the chessboard, each character in this grand drama, plays a role. Their strengths and weaknesses, unique movements, and capabilities all contribute to the game's flow. The humble yet useful pawn, the powerful queen, the all-important king, and every piece in between have a part to play in this intricate narrative that unfolds on the 64 squares of a chessboard.

Pawns

Pawns represent the infantry soldiers who populated the vast armies of the past. These foot soldiers, the backbone of any military force, were essential in warfare, just as pawns are in a game of chess.

Each player begins with eight pawns, arranged on the second row (for white) and the seventh row (for black) of the 8x8 chessboard. These pawns symbolize the rank-and-file soldiers who were often the most numerous in any army.

Historically, soldiers like these were usually not highly ranked or particularly well-armed, but their sheer numbers and collective strength were crucial to the success of military operations.

3. *Pawns represent soldiers in any army. Source: https://unsplash.com/photos/nAjil1z3eLk?utm_source=unsplash& utm_medium=referral&utm_content=creditShareLink*

Pawn Moves and Captures

In chess, pawns have unique movement and capturing abilities. They are the only pieces that move and capture in different ways.

1. **Movement:** A pawn moves straight forward, but only one square at a time, except for its very first move. On its first move, a pawn has the option of moving forward one or two squares. However, it's important to note that this is a one-time option. Once the pawn has moved, whether it has moved one square or two, it can only move one square at a

time for the rest of the game. The pawn is the only piece that cannot move backward or sideways.

4. A pawn can only move forward. Source: https://images.chesscomfiles.com/uploads/v1/images_users/tiny_ mce/pdrpnht/phpEH1kWv.png

2. **Capturing:** Unlike its typical forward movement, a pawn captures diagonally. If an opponent's piece is on an adjacent diagonal square in front of the pawn, the pawn can capture that piece by moving to that square. Think of it like a soldier lunging with a sword or spear to strike down an adversary.

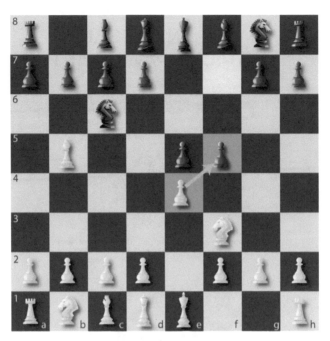

5. Pawns capture diagonally. Source:
*https://images.chesscomfiles.com/uploads/v1/images_users/tiny_*
mce/pdrpnht/phpvXSs5p.png

3. **Special Moves:** There are two special moves associated with pawns: "en passant" and "promotion."

   • **En Passant (French for "passing"):** This is a special capturing move that's only available under specific circumstances. If a pawn moves two squares forward from its starting position and lands next to an opponent's pawn, the opponent has the option to capture the first player's pawn as if it had only moved one square forward.

EN PASSANT:
TRICKY PAWN CAPTURE

WHEN A PAWN MOVES TWO SQUARES FROM ITS INITIAL POSITION AND
PASSES A SQUARE CONTROLLED BY AN ENEMY PAWN, THE ENEMY PAWN
CAN CAPTURE IT. THE PAWN GETS CAPTURED AS IF IT HAD ONLY MOVED ONE
SQUARE. THIS MOVE IS CALLED "EN PASSANT" WHICH MEANS "IN PASSING".

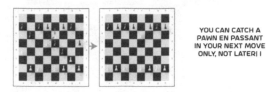

YOU CAN CATCH A
PAWN EN PASSANT
IN YOUR NEXT MOVE
ONLY, NOT LATER! I

THE BLACK PAWN IS GOING TO CAPTURE THE WHITE PAWN EN PASSANT. ON
WHICH SQUARE WILL IT LAND AFTER THE CAPTURE? CHECK THE CORRECT
ANSWER.

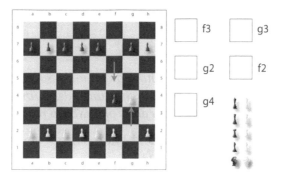

☐ f3   ☐ g3

☐ g2   ☐ f2

☐ g4

6. *The "En Passant" move can only be played with pawns. Source:
https://media.kidsacademy.mobi/worksheets/preview/en-passant-
tricky-pawn-capture.png*

- **Promotion:** This special rule applies when a pawn reaches the last row of the opposite side of the board. When this happens, the pawn is "promoted" and can be exchanged for a queen, rook, bishop, or knight of the same color. This rule symbolizes the potential for an ordinary foot soldier to rise through the ranks and become a powerful figure in the army.

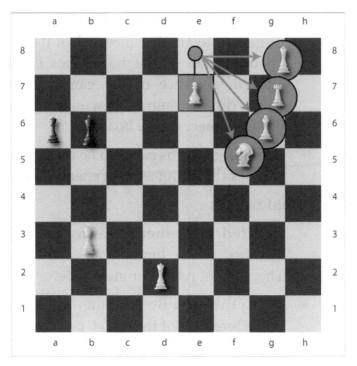

7. *Pawns can be promoted when they reach the last row of the board.*
Source: https://assets.dized.app/project/89d5f752-f681-4c0f-aa2e-
3c0cfac544c0/en-
US/773df2f0a4821d9286ca88a92e4eaf6c/4c6fa975-c21d-47eb-
9b5d-1731bc29cc5e-d41d8cd98f00b204e9800998ecf8427e.png

Strengths and Weaknesses

The pawn, like the infantry soldiers it represents, has strengths and weaknesses on the chess battlefield.

1. Strengths

- **Numbers:** Pawns are the most numerous pieces on the board, and this can be a significant advantage. They can be used to create defensive structures around the more valuable pieces and form "pawn chains" to control the center of the board.

- **Promotion:** The ability of a pawn to be promoted to another piece when it reaches the opposite side of the board can dramatically alter the balance of the game. A promoted pawn can become a new queen, the most powerful piece on the board.

- **Blocking:** Pawns can also be used strategically to block the movements of enemy pieces.

2. **Weaknesses**

- **Limited Movement:** Pawns can only move forward, which limits their maneuverability. They cannot retreat or move sideways.

- **Vulnerability:** Because they are often placed at the forefront of the game, pawns can be easy targets for capture.

- **Isolation:** If a pawn becomes isolated (no pawns on adjacent squares), it can be weaker and more susceptible to capture.

Bishops

In the ancient version of chess, the pieces we now call bishops are often associated with elephant riders or "elephants." Chess has a long history, dating as far as the 6th century in northern India, where it was known as "chaturanga." In this early version of the game, the piece that would become the bishop was often depicted as an elephant and its rider. Due to their size and strength, the elephants were used in warfare just like armored tanks are used today.

As the game spread westward, these "elephants" evolved into the bishops used today. This was partly because the

Western world was less familiar with war elephants. The name "bishop" was coined because the piece's pointed top resembled a bishop's miter, a type of hat used in the Christian church.

8. *Bishops used to symbolize elephant riders in the past. Source: MichaelMaggs, CC BY-SA 2.5 <https://creativecommons.org/licenses/by-sa/2.5>, via Wikimedia Commons: https://commons.wikimedia.org/wiki/File:Chess_piece_-_White_bishop.JPG*

Bishop's Diagonal Move Pattern

Unlike other pieces, which can move in straight lines or L-shaped patterns, the bishop moves diagonally. It can only remain on the color of the square that it started the game on. If it starts on a white square, it will always be on white squares; if it starts on a black square, it will always be on black squares. This is sometimes referred to as the bishop's "color binding."

The bishop can move as many squares as it likes in a diagonal line as long as its path is unobstructed by other pieces. The bishop captures an opponent's piece by landing on the square that the piece occupies.

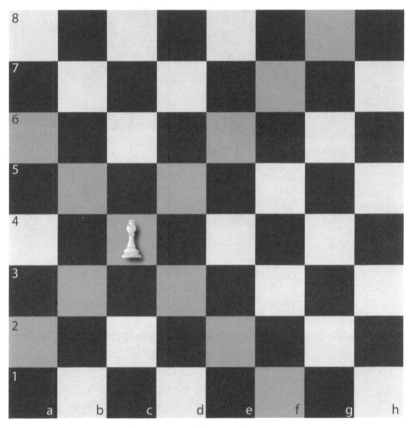

9. Bishops move diagonally. Source:
*https://images.chesscomfiles.com/uploads/v1/images_users/tiny_*
mce/PeterDoggers/phpdzgpdQ.png

Strengths and Weaknesses

Like the elephant riders it symbolizes, the bishop possesses unique strengths and weaknesses on the chess battlefield.

1. Strengths

- **Range:** The bishop can move any number of squares diagonally as long as its path is clear. This allows it to control long stretches of the board and apply pressure from a distance.

- **Pairing:** The two Bishops work well together because they can cover both colors of squares on the board (one bishop is bound to the white squares, and the other to the black squares).

- **Speed:** Bishops can quickly move across the board, especially in open positions where many squares are unoccupied.

2. Weaknesses

- **Color Binding:** Each bishop is restricted to one color of squares (either white or black). This limits its control over the board and can sometimes make it less effective.

- **Blocked Paths:** If the game's position is closed, meaning many squares are occupied by pawns, a bishop's movement can be severely hampered.

- **Vulnerability:** Similar to pawns, bishops can become easy targets for capture, especially if they are caught on the edge of the board with limited escape routes.

Knights

The knights, depicted on the chessboard as a horse's head, symbolize the gallant and swift cavalry horsemen of medieval times. Just like real-life knights, these chess pieces are known for their exceptional mobility and prowess on the battlefield. They were highly regarded for their courage and skillful maneuvers during medieval warfare.

10. Knights symbolize the horsemen of medieval times. Source: che (production: Nolanus, lighting assistance: Danny B.), CC BY-SA 2.5 <https://creativecommons.org/licenses/by-sa/2.5>, via Wikimedia Commons: https://commons.wikimedia.org/wiki/File:Chess_knight_0971.jpg

Knight's Unique "L-shaped" Move

One of the most distinctive features of the knight is its unique move. Unlike any other chess piece, the knight moves in a particular "L-shaped" pattern. It advances one or two squares in any direction—forward, backward, left, or right—and then makes a sharp turn to the left or right, moving one square perpendicular to its previous direction if it moved two at the start and two squares if it moved one. This allows the knight to jump over other pieces, making it the only chess piece that can bypass obstacles directly in its path.

The knight's "L-shaped" move gives it a remarkable chessboard advantage. It can swiftly navigate across the entire board, reaching places that other pieces might find difficult to access. This ability grants the knight a reputation for being a master of surprise attacks and unexpected maneuvers. It can catch opponents off guard, making it a valuable asset in a player's strategy.

11. The knight moves in an L-shape. Source: https://images.chesscomfiles.com/uploads/v1/images_users/tiny_ mce/pdrpnht/phpVuLl4W.png

Strengths and Weaknesses

1. Strengths

- **Versatility:** The knight's unique move allows it to reach different parts of the board, making it a versatile piece. It can swiftly change its position to support other pieces or launch attacks from unexpected angles.

- **Attack and Defense:** The knight's move enables it to attack multiple squares simultaneously, making it a potent offensive weapon. Additionally, its ability to jump over other pieces makes it an excellent defender, as it can intercept opponents' moves that other pieces cannot.

- **Forks:** The knight's move is especially useful for executing tactical strategies like forks. A fork occurs when the knight threatens two or more pieces simultaneously, forcing the opponent to make a difficult decision.

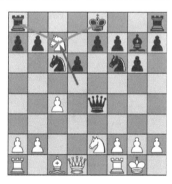

12. A fork occurs when a knight threatens two pieces simultaneously.
Source: I, Alex valavanis, CC BY-SA 3.0
<http://creativecommons.org/licenses/by-sa/3.0/>, via Wikimedia Commons:
https://commons.wikimedia.org/wiki/File:Chess_fork_knight_che ssbase.svg

2. Weaknesses

- **Limited Range**: Although the knight is a versatile piece, it does have a limitation in terms of range. Unlike the queen or rook, which can move across the entire board in one move, the knight's reach is relatively limited. It takes several moves for a knight to traverse from one side of the board to the other.

- **Vulnerability to Attacks:** Due to its unique move, the knight can sometimes find itself in vulnerable positions. Other pieces, particularly pawns, can target the squares adjacent to the knight, making it challenging to escape or defend itself.

- **Complex Strategies:** Mastering the knight's unique move requires practice and strategic thinking. It may take time for young chess players to fully grasp the intricacies of the knight's movement patterns and incorporate them effectively into their overall strategy.

Rooks

The rook, known as a castle, has been used to represent the chariot drivers in medieval times. It is a valuable piece because of its ability to move in a straight line, horizontally or vertically, as far as it wants, as long as there are no other pieces in its path.

13. Rooks represent the chariot drivers in medieval times. Source: MichaelMaggs, CC BY-SA 2.5 <https://creativecommons.org/licenses/by-sa/2.5>, via Wikimedia Commons: https://commons.wikimedia.org/wiki/File:Chess_piece_-_White_rook.JPG

Rook's Straight-Line Move

The rook's straight-line move is one of its greatest strengths. Unlike other pieces, the rook can move in a straight line as far as it wants, either horizontally or vertically, as long as there are no other pieces in its path. This makes it a very valuable piece to have, as it can quickly move across the board and attack the opponent's pieces.

The rook's straight-line move is also useful in controlling the center of the board. Since it can move in a straight line, it can control a lot of squares at once, making it difficult for the opponent to move their pieces around.

14. Rooks move in a straight-line. Source: https://images.chesscomfiles.com/uploads/v1/images_users/tiny_ mce/pdrpnht/phpfyINI1.png

Strengths and Weaknesses

1. Strengths

- **Long-Range Move**: The rook's long-range move allows it to attack the opponent's pieces from far away, making it difficult for the opponent to defend.

- **Control of the Center**: The rook's ability to move in a straight line allows it to control a lot of squares at once, making it difficult for the opponent to move their pieces around.

- **Endgame Power:** The rook is particularly useful in the endgame when there are fewer pieces on the board. Its long-range moves can be used to checkmate the opposing king.

2. Weaknesses

- **Blocked by Other Pieces:** The rook is not very effective in the opening stages of the game because it is usually blocked by other pieces. Players must be careful not to move their rooks too soon in a game, or they may be trapped in a corner of the board and unable to move.

- **Cannot Jump Over Other Pieces**: The rook can only move in straight lines and cannot jump over other pieces.

In addition to its strengths and weaknesses, the rook has a special move called castling. Castling involves moving the king two spaces towards a rook and then moving the rook to the square next to the king on the opposite side. This move is used to protect the king and to bring the rook into play.

Queen

The queen is the most powerful piece on the chessboard. It can move in any direction, horizontally, vertically, or diagonally, as far as it wants, as long as there are no other pieces in its path. This makes the queen very valuable, as it can control a lot of squares on the board and attack the opponent's pieces from many different angles.

The queen is also a very important defensive piece. It can be used to protect the king and other pieces on the board and control the center of the board.

15. The queen is the most powerful chess piece. Source: MichaelMaggs, CC BY-SA 2.5 <https://creativecommons.org/licenses/by-sa/2.5>, via Wikimedia Commons: https://commons.wikimedia.org/wiki/File:Chess_piece_-_White_queen.jpg

The Queen's Combination of Bishop and Rook Moves

The queen's unique combination of moves is what makes it such a powerful piece. It can move like a bishop, diagonally across the board, as well as like a rook, in a straight line horizontally or vertically.

The queen's diagonal moves are particularly useful for attacking the opponent's pieces and controlling the center of the board. On the other hand, its straight-line moves are useful for attacking the opponent's pawns and protecting other pieces on the board.

16. The queen can move diagonally, horizontally, vertically, or in a square. Source: https://images.chesscomfiles.com/uploads/v1/images_users/tiny_mce/pdrpnht/phpCQgsYR.png

Strengths and Weaknesses

1. Strengths

- **Versatility:** The queen's ability to move in any direction makes it a very versatile piece on the board. It can attack the opponent's pieces from many different angles and control a lot of squares on the board.

- **Offensive Power:** The queen is a very powerful offensive piece. Its diagonal moves allow it to attack the opponent's pieces from far away, while its straight-line moves allow it to attack the opponent's pawns and protect other pieces on the board.

- **Defensive Capabilities:** The queen is also a very important defensive piece. It can be used to protect the king and other pieces on the board.

2. **Weaknesses**

- **Vulnerability:** Because the queen is such a powerful piece, it is often a target for the opponent's attacks. Players must be careful not to leave it in a vulnerable position.

- **Limited Mobility in the Opening:** Since the queen is such a powerful piece, it is often targeted by the opponent's pieces in the opening stages of the game. Players must be careful not to move their queen too early, or it may become trapped.

King

The king is the most important piece on the chessboard. It is the only piece that cannot be captured, and the game's primary objective is to checkmate the opponent's king. If a player's king is checkmated, the game is over, and that player loses.

Seeing how vulnerable to attack the king is from the opponent's pieces, it must be protected at all times. In fact, the king's vulnerability is what makes the game of chess so interesting and challenging.

17. The king is the most important piece on the chessboard. Source: MichaelMaggs, CC BY-SA 2.5 <https://creativecommons.org/licenses/by-sa/2.5>, via Wikimedia Commons: https://commons.wikimedia.org/wiki/File:Chess_piece_-_White_king.jpg

King's Limited Moves

The king's moves are very limited. It can only move one square in any direction, horizontally, vertically, or diagonally. It cannot move very far on the board and must rely on other pieces to protect it.

The king's limited moves are what make it such an important piece. It cannot be moved into a position where the opponent's pieces will capture it and must always be protected by the other pieces on the board.

18. The king has limited moves. Source:
*https://images.chesscomfiles.com/uploads/v1/images_users/tiny_*
mce/pdrpnht/phpmVRKYr.png

The Primary Objective Is to Protect the King

The primary objective of the game of chess is to checkmate the opponent's king. This means that the opponent's king must be put in a position where it is under attack and cannot move out of danger.

Protecting the king is the most important aspect of the game. If a player's king is not protected, it can be captured by the opponent's pieces, and the game is over. Players must be careful not to leave their king in a vulnerable position and must always be thinking about how to protect it.

In addition to protecting the king, players must also be thinking about how to attack the opponent's king. This can be done by using other pieces on the board to create threats and force the opponent's king into a vulnerable position.

CHESS BOARD SETUP

19. *Setting up your board correctly will help you play. Source:*
https://www.cyruscrafts.com/img/cms/blog/play-
chess/chess%20board%20setup.jpg

Key Takeaways

- Each chess piece has a unique role representing a division of the military from ancient times.

- Pawns represent infantry soldiers and have limited movement but become powerful when promoted to other pieces.

- Bishops represent elephant riders and move diagonally, controlling half of the board. Two bishops pair well together.

- Knights represent cavalry horsemen and move in an L-shaped pattern, jumping over other pieces. They are masters of surprise attacks.

- Rooks represent chariot drivers and can move any number of spaces horizontally or vertically as long as the path is clear. They can control much of the board.

- The queen combines the movement possibilities of bishops and rooks, making it the most versatile and powerful piece.

- The king is the most important piece, and the objective of the game is to checkmate the opponent's king. The king has the most limited movement.

- Each piece has its own strengths and weaknesses related to movement, maneuverability, range, control of the board, vulnerability to attack, and role in attack/defense strategies.

- Together, the pieces work as a team to protect the king while trying to checkmate the opponent. Each piece plays a crucial part in the grand narrative of the game.

Chapter 3: Chess Notation: The Language of Chess

One of the most important skills to learn when playing chess is reading and understanding chess notation.

Chess notation is a system where symbols are used to record and describe each move made during a game. This notation is used to record both players' moves and refer back to them during a game or to analyze the game later. It is also used to communicate chess moves between players.

Standard Chess Notation/Algebraic Notation

Algebraic notation is a system used to record and describe the moves in a game of chess. It is used to accurately record each move, including the pieces moved, their starting and ending squares, and any special moves such as castling.

Algebraic notation is based on a coordinate system. Each square on the chessboard is assigned a letter and number combination. The vertical columns of the board are labeled with the letters a-h, from left to right. The horizontal rows of the board are numbered 1-8, from bottom to top.

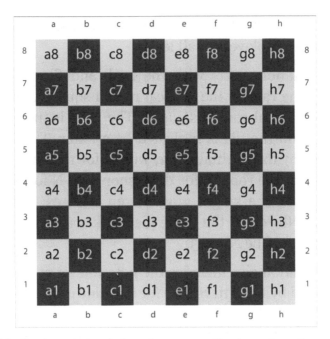

20. Algebraic notation is based on a coordinate system. Source: https://chessily.com/wp-content/uploads/2022/05/chess-notation-diagram.png

To record a move, the piece moved is identified by its initial letter. For example, a knight is identified by the letter N. Then, the starting square of the piece is noted, followed by the ending square. For example, Nf3 means that the knight moved from the f-file to the 3rd rank.

Special moves, such as castling or capturing a piece, are indicated by additional symbols. For castling, the letter O is used to represent the king moving two squares. For example, O-O stands for kingside castling, and O-O-O stands for queenside castling. Captures are indicated by the letter x. For example, Nxf3 means that the knight captured a piece on the f3 square.

Algebraic notation is a simple yet effective way to record and describe the moves in a game of chess. This notation allows chess games to be accurately documented and easily understood by players of all levels.

The notation starts with the rank and file of the piece moving. The rank is the vertical row of squares, and the file is the horizontal row of squares. The rank is indicated by a number, and the file is indicated by a letter. The pieces are identified by their initial letter, with K for the king, Q for the queen, R for the rook, B for the bishop, and N for the knight. For example, if a knight moves from b1 to c3, the notation would be Nb1-c3. If the same piece takes a piece on c3, the notation would be Nb1xc3.

The notation also includes the notation for castling, which is indicated by the letters O-O for kingside castling, and O-O-O for queenside castling. The notation also includes the notation for pawn promotion. When a pawn reaches the 8th rank, it can be promoted to a higher piece, such as a queen or a rook. This is indicated by the pawn's initial letter followed by an equals (=) sign and the initial letter of the promoted piece. For example, if a pawn on e7 is promoted to a queen, the notation would be e=7Q.

Numeric Notations

This system of notation uses numbers to represent moves, allowing players to quickly and accurately record all the moves of a game.

In numeric notation, each square on the chessboard is assigned a number from 1 to 64. The numbers are arranged in an 8x8 grid, with the a-file on the left (1-8) and the h-file on the right (57-64). Players can then record moves by referring to the squares that pieces move from and to. For example, if a pawn moves from e4 to e5, it would be recorded as 32-40.

This system of notation has several advantages for chess players. It is very concise, allowing players to quickly record moves and review games. It is also easy to learn. Furthermore, it is very accurate, as it eliminates the possibility of ambiguity when recording moves.

In addition to recording moves, numeric notation can also be used to analyze games. Players can use the numbers to identify patterns and trends in their games and to quickly spot mistakes. This can be especially useful for studying openings and endgames.

Annotated Games

Annotated games are a great way for chess players to improve. These are games that have been analyzed by experienced chess players and annotated with detailed comments. These comments can include detailed explanations of why a certain move was made and assessments of the position. By studying annotated games, players can learn from the mistakes of others and gain insight into the thought processes of experienced players.

Annotated games are especially useful for players who are just starting out in chess. By studying annotated games, they can learn the game's basics and better understand the strategic elements. They can also learn to recognize patterns and develop tactics to help them in their games.

Annotated games can also be helpful for more experienced players. By studying annotated games, they can learn new strategies and tactics and gain insight into the thought processes of experienced players. This can help them become more successful in their own games.

Annotated games are a great way for players of all levels to improve their game. By studying annotated games, players can learn from the mistakes of others and gain insight into the thought processes of experienced players. They can also learn new strategies and tactics, as well as gain a better understanding of the strategic elements of the game.

Small diagrams next to each notation example visually demonstrate how that system works. For algebraic notation, you could show a knight moving from b1 to c3 marked as Nb1-c3. For numeric notation, you could show the grid with numbering and mark a sample move.

Descriptive Notation

Descriptive Notation is a simple and effective way of recording chess moves. It uses a standard set of symbols and abbreviations to describe each move. For example, a move of a pawn to a new square is written as "P-e4" (e4 being the square the pawn moves to). Similarly, a move of a knight to a new square is written as "N-f3" (f3 being the square the knight moves to).

The advantage of Descriptive Notation is that it is easy to understand and follow. It is also easy to read back a game from the notation, allowing for a better understanding of the game.

Despite its popularity, there are some drawbacks to Descriptive Notation. For example, some moves, such as castling or en passant, are difficult to describe in the notation. Also, the notation can be difficult to read for those who are not familiar with it.

Variations Annotations

Variations are a type of annotation that is used to record different lines of play that could have been taken in the game. They are useful for analyzing the game, as they provide a way to explore different possibilities that may have been available. Variations can also be used to study openings, endgames, and other strategic ideas.

Annotations can be used to record different tactical ideas or strategies that may have been used in the game. They can also be used to record the thought processes of the players, as well as mistakes that were made during the game.

Annotations can be used to help improve your understanding of the game. They can be used to review games that have been played, as well as to learn from mistakes that have been made. They can also be used to help develop new strategies and ideas.

Variations and annotations are an important part of learning and improving the game of chess. They can be used to study openings, endgames, and other strategic ideas, as well as to review games and learn from mistakes. They can also help to develop new ideas and strategies.

Power of Chess Notation

The power of chess notation is often underestimated, yet it is an essential tool for any chess player. Recording moves allow players to review their games, analyze their mistakes, and learn from them. It also allows players to share their games with friends and colleagues or even publish them for the world to see.

Chess notation is a valuable resource for any chess player, regardless of their level. By recording the moves of a game, players can look back and identify mistakes that they may have made. This allows them to review their own games and identify areas for improvement. Additionally, chess notation allows players to share their games with others and receive feedback from more experienced players. This can be a great learning opportunity, as it allows players to learn from the mistakes of others.

It can also be used to review the games of famous players. By studying the moves of chess masters, players can learn a great deal about the game. This can be a great way for players to improve their own game, as they can gain insights from those who have mastered the game.

Finally, chess notation can be used to publish games for the world to see. This can be a great way to get feedback from other players, as well as to showcase one's own skills.

Key Takeaways

- Precisely record every move made during a game. This allows players to review and analyze their games, identify mistakes, and find areas for improvement.

- Communicate moves to others. Chess notation provides a common language that allows players to share and discuss their moves and analyze games together. This allows them to learn from each other.

- Study and learn from annotated games. Analyzed games with explanatory comments provide insight into strong players' strategies and thought processes. This teaches students tactics, techniques, and strategic planning.

- Publish games for discussion. Players can publish their games for others to review and provide feedback. This helps them improve through critiques from more experienced players.

- Identify patterns and recurring mistakes. By reviewing notated games, players can spot trends in their own gameplay that reveal weaknesses they need to improve. They can then focus their practice on addressing these issues.

- Learn from chess history. Studying famous games and annotative commentaries teaches players about pivotal historical moments that shaped the understanding of strategy and technique.

Chapter 4: The Top Ten Tips Needed in Chess

1. Awareness

Awareness is very important in chess. You need to be aware of the moves your opponent is making, no matter how insignificant they seem at first. A player who does not pay close attention to their opponent's moves will have a lot of trouble.

21. You have to be aware of your opponent's moves. Source:
https://unsplash.com/photos/IsphRwNKkjc?utm_source=unsp
lash&utm_medium=referral&utm_content=creditShareLink

If you are not watching every move your opponent makes, you will miss opportunities to gain an advantage. The opponent might set a trap into which the unaware player falls. The opponent's strategy might develop and strengthen before you notice. You may miss chances to make powerful moves of yourself because you were not observing what your opponent was doing.

You develop awareness through practice. You can work on visualization and mental chess exercises to improve your pattern recognition. By reviewing past games and analyzing where you missed opportunities, you can learn to spot subtle threats and possibilities on the board. Getting feedback from instructors and more experienced players also helps improve awareness.

During a game, you must maintain awareness the entire time. You can take notes of important changes on the board. You can set reminders to re-analyze the position periodically. You should actively try to visualize possible next moves by your opponent. You need to stay focused and alert to catch whatever develops on the board.

Awareness of the opponent's moves is essential for you to take advantage of tactical opportunities, avoid blunders, and gain an edge in the game. You must train yourself to maintain a high level of alertness and observation throughout the entire chess game.

2. Make the Best Possible Move

Making the best possible move is important in chess. With each move, you should aim to make the move that has the most advantage. Every move counts!

In chess, every move you make has consequences. It either weakens your position, strengthens your position, or keeps it the same. You always want to make the move that strengthens your position the most or weakens your opponent's the most.

Even seemingly insignificant moves can turn the tide of the game. A move that first appears unimportant might actually open up an advantage you didn't see earlier. So, you shouldn't dismiss any moves without carefully analyzing them.

To find the best move, take your time and consider all of your options. Look for moves that threaten your opponent's pieces, moves that develop your pieces, and moves that prevent threats from your opponent. Imagine how your opponent might respond and which moves leave you in a better position after their response.

The perfect move might not exist on the chessboard. But with careful thinking and analysis, you can find a move that gives you the biggest advantage and improves your chances of winning the game. Making the best possible move on each turn is an important skill that will help you become a stronger chess player.

So, on every move, focus on finding a way to improve your position, threaten your opponent, and make it harder for your opponent to achieve their goals. This focus will help you make the move that gives you the biggest edge and brings you closer to checkmate!

---

3. Be a Master Planner

Being a master planner is essential in chess. Every move you make should be well thought out and part of an overarching plan to win the game. Any move you make without proper planning is a mistake waiting to happen.

In chess, you have to think several moves in advance. For each move you make, you should consider how your opponent might respond and how you will respond to their response. Effective planning requires you to visualize multiple lines of play and calculate which leads to the best outcomes for you.

You develop your planning skills through practice and training. When first starting out, take your time to plan each move. Carefully examine the board, consider your options, and think through the possible consequences of each option. Even for seemingly unimportant moves, take a moment to ensure the move does not weaken your position or open yourself up to attacks.

As you gain experience, you will develop the ability to quickly spot important strategic possibilities on the board. You'll start planning multiple move sequences in your head to determine the best course of action. But proper planning always remains essential, now just happening more quickly due to your improved chess vision.

As you play, get in the habit of planning for the next 3-5 moves. Ask yourself, "What is my plan for winning the game?", "What threats do I need to avoid?", "How can I improve my pieces' positions?" A general game plan will give context to your individual moves and help ensure they work together toward victory.

Proper planning and thinking ahead are key skills that every strong chess player has mastered. With practice and experience, you'll develop the ability to quickly spot strategic possibilities and plan multiple move sequences to achieve your objectives. But you must start every game by making a firm commitment to plan carefully for each and every move.

---

4. Know the Worth of Each Piece

Knowing the relative worth of each piece is fundamental. Although all pieces move and capture in different ways, they do not have equal value. Understanding the worth of each piece will help you make good trades, calculate attack chances, and determine an optimal strategy.

King = ? points   Bishops = 3 points

Queen = 9 points   Knights= 3 points

Rooks = 5 points   Powns= 1 point

22. Knowing the value of each piece can help you plan the best strategy.
Source :
https://miro.medium.com/v2/resize:fit:598/1*2p5MoHoxFgZkdplj OK6CuQ.png

The pieces, in order from most valuable to least, are:

- The queen is the most powerful piece. It can move any number of squares horizontally, vertically, or diagonally. So, losing your queen usually means losing the game.

- The two rooks are next in value. Rooks can move any number of squares in a horizontal or vertical line. Having both rooks working together on an open file can create devastating attacks.

- The two bishops are slightly less valuable than the rooks. However, bishops often become more powerful in endgames due to their ability to control more of the board.

- The two knights are next in value. Knights have the unique ability to jump over other pieces. While generally less powerful than bishops, knights often become more valuable in closed positions.

- The eight pawns have the least value. However, advanced pawns, especially passed pawns, significantly increase in worth and have the chance to be promoted to a more powerful piece.

The relative worth of the pieces helps inform many decisions you make in chess. When considering trades, you want to exchange lower value for higher value pieces when possible. When seeking mating attacks, you aim first for the opponent's most valuable pieces. And when devising an endgame strategy, understanding which remaining pieces are strongest helps you achieve victory.

5. Learn Quickly on the Job

Learning quickly "on the job" is essential for chess improvement. While studying chess theory and opening lines is important, nothing teaches you more than actual play. A chess player must be willing to expose their ideas to testing during real games and learn from the results.

When you first start playing, almost everything you learn will come from your own games. Each new position encountered on the board will teach you something about how pieces work together, tactical motifs, and strategic planning. Pay close attention to these lessons and analyze your games thoroughly to identify mistakes and things you can improve.

Even experienced players continue to learn enormously from each game they play. Every opponent presents a new and unique testing ground for your ideas. You'll likely encounter unusual tactics or unfamiliar strategies that challenge your preconceptions. Paying careful attention to these new situations allows you to quickly expand your knowledge and understanding.

After your games, take time to analyze where you went wrong and what you can do better next time. Look for lessons in superior tactics, efficient development, useful strategic maneuvers, and more effective plans. Commit these lessons to memory so that you can apply them the next time a similar position arises.

Over time, experiences from your own practice games and tournaments will build up your chess wisdom far beyond what you could gain from only books and theory. This hard-earned practical knowledge – built through patience, effort, and a willingness to learn from mistakes – will elevate you to a higher level among your peers.

Playing actual games and learning from your results provides an unrivaled education in chess. You'll quickly accumulate wisdom about piece coordination, identifying key threats, effective development, midgame plans, endgame techniques, and much more. View each new game as an opportunity to gain practical lessons that will immediately improve your play.

6. Take Charge of the Center

Controlling the center is a key principle in chess. The four central squares – d4, e4, d5, and e5 – are strategically important. A piece that occupies a central square has more potential to influence the game compared to pieces on the sides of the board.

There are a few reasons why controlling the center is advantageous. First, pieces in the center have more potential moves. They can attack in more directions or move toward either side of the board. This mobility gives central pieces more influence over the game.

Second, central pawns that have advanced are more difficult for the opponent to capture. Since they control important space and block opponent pieces, central pawns provide a strong foundation for the rest of your pieces.

Third, controlling the center often allows you to put pressure on your opponent's pieces. Since pieces on the sides have fewer possible moves, central domination can confine and limit their activity. This passivity by your opponent plays into your hands.

While controlling the center is important, achieving it is not always easy. Your opponent will likely also want to occupy central squares. You may need to sacrifice the development of other pieces or make advances with your pawns to gain the upper hand in the center.

Once you control the center, you must utilize central dominance effectively. Attack your opponent's pieces, aim for central outposts for your knights and bishops, and seek pawn breaks that further restrict your opponent's positioning. But avoid leaving central pieces undefended where they can be captured.

Occupying and controlling the central squares is desirable for its many tangible and intangible advantages. While achieving central control requires effort, maintaining and maximizing its benefits will put you in a strong strategic position to wrest the initiative from your opponent and gain the upper hand.

---

7. Protecting the King

Protecting the king is of utmost importance in chess. The goal of the game is to checkmate the opponent's king, so keeping your own king safe should be your top priority. Even one mistake that leaves the king vulnerable could cost you the game.

From the start of the game, you should develop your pieces to defend the king. Pieces that can easily guard important squares near the king should be developed first. Meanwhile, avoid making pawn moves that could weaken squares around the king.

As the middlegame unfolds, constantly monitor threats toward your king and make necessary moves to defend against them. Be aware of any sacrificial attacks that could expose your king, as even cheap sacrifices can become deadly if your king is unprotected. Always keep at least one defender near the king that can provide protection against discovered attacks.

In the endgame, the king often needs to become more active to win. But take any advance with caution. Before moving the king into the center of the board, make sure all attackers are removed and no opponent pieces are lurking to give a check. Once the king moves forward, find ways to block enemy checks while advancing toward checkmate.

Throughout the game, follow basic guidelines to keep your king safe:

1. Control squares directly in front of the king.

2. Keep at least one pawn on the file in front of the king.

3. Place a minor piece (knight or bishop) near the king to provide protection.

4. Avoid moving the king unnecessarily unless you are ready to expose it to bait the opponent.

While aggressive play is often required to win, never sacrifice material or expose your king unless a concrete plan leads to checkmate. Protecting your king should always be your default approach in unclear positions. After all, one check can end the game instantly, so vigilance in defense pays the highest dividend in chess.

Safeguarding the king should be a top priority throughout the entire game. Good king safety at the start will reduce threats in the middlegame, and proper precautions in the endgame will allow you to advance toward victory without falling into desperation tactics by your opponent. Keeping the king protected will give you the license you need to outplay your opponent in all other aspects of the game.

8. Understanding Timing

Understanding proper timing is an important skill in chess. Knowing when to make certain types of moves – trades, attacks, sacrifices, advances – can make the difference between winning and losing. Players must develop a feel for the right moment to execute various strategies.

23. Understanding proper timing is an important chess skill. Source : https://unsplash.com/photos/xfNeB1stZ_0?utm_source=unsplash &utm_medium=referral&utm_content=creditShareLink

When trading pieces, the timing needs to be right to gain maximum advantage. Trading a piece too early may be premature, while trading too late may allow your opponent to gain counter play. The best trades often happen when your opponent's piece is temporally placed in a vulnerable position.

Before launching an attack, players must gauge whether the moment is right. Waiting too long can allow your opponent to improve their position while moving too soon could expose your pieces before they are optimally placed. Attacks tend to have the highest chance of success when your opponent's pieces are not coordinated.

Making sacrifices also requires a sense of good timing. Sacrificing a piece early often offers too little, while doing so too late may allow your opponent to recapture material easily. Ideal moments for sacrifices often occur when your opponent is overwhelmed defending against threats.

Advancing pawns also needs to be done at the proper time. Advancing too soon can weaken your position, while delaying too long could give your opponent chances to blockade. The best pawn moves often happen when your opponent's pieces are tied down elsewhere.

Players must develop an intuitive feeling for when certain types of moves will be most effective. This comes with experience and analyzing where good and bad timing hurt or helped your gameplay. With experience, you'll start to recognize optimal moments for trades, attacks, sacrifices, and advances, allowing you to execute your plans at the right time and maximize your chances of success.

9. Having the End Game in View

Having the endgame in view from the very start is crucial. Every decision you make in the opening and middle game should be made with the potential endgame in mind. Keeping the endgame as your ultimate goal will help you make strategic moves that set you up for success at the end of the game.

In the opening, select moves that develop your pieces with an eye toward the endgame. Avoid moves that control the center at the expense of developing your minor pieces, which tend to be stronger in endgames with few pawns. Instead, focus on positioning your knights and bishops onto good squares from which they can be effective later.

In the middlegame, trading off minor pieces and pawns when advantageous can simplify the position and bring you closer to an endgame where your remaining pieces may excel. Look for exchanges that retain pawns on the same side of the board, which are often useful in creating passed pawns and delivering checkmates.

As you analyze potential attacks and sacrifices, consider how they would impact an eventual endgame. Moves that leave you with fewer pieces after an attack may be unwise, while those that trade-off your opponent's stronger pieces can set you up well.

Even just keeping the endgame possibilities in the back of your mind can subtly influence decisions throughout the game. Many moves that seem irrational in the middlegame make perfect sense when viewed as preparations for an eventual endgame.

The best chess players plan their route to victory from the very start of the game. Maneuvers that appear dubious in the opening and middlegame are often understandable when seen as strategic preparations for a favorable endgame. Keep your ultimate goal in mind with every move, and make decisions that improve your chances of converting any lead into a checkmate.

10. Always Be on Guard

Always remaining on guard is essential in chess, even when occupying an advantageous position. It is natural for players to become less vigilant once they have an advantage, but dropping one's guard is a surefire way to lose what seemed like a winning position. Maintaining full alertness and caution from start to finish is the mark of a strong player.

Overconfidence can creep in and cause players to make careless mistakes when gaining an advantage. They may rush moves or fail to calculate tactics carefully. But even small inaccuracies can give the opponent counter play and start chipping away at your lead. Never assume that you have won the game until you checkmate your opponent's king.

The stronger your position becomes, the more tempting it is to relax. But this is exactly when your vigilance should increase. Your opponent will become more desperate and likely to launch unexpected or sacrificial attacks. You must keep a watchful eye out for any sneaky tactics that could turn the tables.

Periodically pause the game and re-examine the position with a critical eye. Ask yourself, "What is my opponent threatening?" and "How can I improve my position further?". Looking for threats and weaknesses in your position will keep you on high alert, even with a significant advantage.

In the endgame, vigilance remains essential. Even the tiniest error can allow your opponent to draw or even win a seemingly won position. As desperation tactics abound, make every pawn move and king advance with extreme care.

Maintaining full focus and vigilance separates the best players from the rest, even when comfortably ahead. Dropping one's guard, no matter the size of the lead, is a recipe for disaster. The most dangerous moments in chess are often when you think you are safest. Staying on high alert from the very first move to the very last is the mark of a true chess master.

Key Takeaways

- You must pay close attention to every move your opponent makes to spot opportunities, traps, and

---

threats. Developing observation skills through practice and review is crucial.

- For each move, aim to make the option that gives you the biggest advantage. Consider all possibilities carefully before deciding. Even small moves can be important.

- Plan several moves ahead to develop a strategy. With experience, you will learn to quickly visualize strategic possibilities and evaluate multiple lines of play. Proper planning is essential for every move.

- Understanding the relative worth of the pieces helps make good trades, calculate attacks, and determine strategy. The most to least valuable are queens, rooks, bishops, knights, and pawns.

- Much of chess knowledge comes from experience gained during actual play. Analyzing your games helps you identify mistakes and things to improve.

- Occupying and controlling the central squares provides advantages like mobility, the foundation for pieces, and pressure on opponents' pieces, but it requires effort to achieve and maintain.

- Your king's safety should always be the top priority. Constantly monitor threats and make necessary defenses. Be more cautious with the king during the endgame.

- Knowing when to make certain moves like trades, attacks, and sacrifices can make a big difference. Good timing comes with experience.

- The best players plan their entire game with the endgame in mind. Maneuvers that seem puzzling often make sense as the endgame approaches.

- Even when comfortably ahead, maintain full focus and caution. Dropping your guard is how you can lose an advantage. Stay alert from start to finish like a true chess master.

Chapter 5: The Golden Laws of Attack and Defense in Chess

Chess requires planning, foresight, and calculation. Understanding attack and defense is crucial for the following reasons:

1. Attack is one of the primary ways to win a game of chess. Players look for ways to attack and threaten the opponent's king to gain the advantage. Understanding how to attack effectively and identifying weaknesses in the opponent's position is important.

2. Knowing how to defend against an attack is just as important. Players need to be able to determine if they are being attacked, assess the strength of the opponent's attack, and devise a defensive plan to stop or minimize the threat.

3. Most positions in chess involve a balance between attack and defense. Players constantly evaluate whether it is more advantageous to attack or defend in a given position. Good attackers also know how to defend and vice versa.

4. Strong attacks often force defensive moves from the opponent, giving the attacker the initiative. However, overextending in an attack can allow counterattacking chances for the defender. This interplay between offense and defense is a core part of chess strategy.

Laws of Attack

1. **Defend Your Pieces First:** Before launching an attack, ensure your pieces are properly defended. An undefended piece can be targeted and captured, disrupting your attack.

2. **Exploit the Weaknesses of Your Opponent:** Look for weaknesses in your opponent's formation, such as undefended pieces, exposed corners or sides, or a lack of coordination between pieces. Target these weaknesses to gain an advantage.

3. **Attempt a Strategic Exchange:** Trade-off pieces that are well-placed for your opponent but inconveniently placed for you. This can give you a positional advantage to launch a successful attack.

4. **Strengthen Your Attack:** Bring more forces to bear on the target of your attack. Concentrate your pieces to build pressure and force defensive concessions from your opponent.

5. **Make Aggressive Moves**: Don't be afraid to sacrifice material if it strengthens your attacking chances. Sacrifices often force defensive moves that allow your remaining forces to overrun your opponent's position.

Types of Attacking Tactics

1. Fork

A fork occurs when one piece attacks (or threatens to capture) two or more of the opponent's pieces at the same time. Forks cause the opponent problems because they have to either defend multiple threats with one move or lose a piece. For example, a bishop forks a queen, and rook forces one of those pieces to move.

A fork is an effective tactical tool because it brings two or more of the opponent's pieces under attack simultaneously, disrupting their position and gaining material. Looking for potential fork threats is an important part of calculating an attack.

2. Pin

A pin occurs when a piece is attacking another piece, and the piece in between cannot be moved without exposing the pinned piece. For example, if a rook is pinned between a bishop and a queen, it cannot move away without the queen being captured.

Pins are useful tactics because they immobilize an opponent's piece, rendering it ineffective for a time. Pins often precede forks and skewers as a way of tying down enemies.

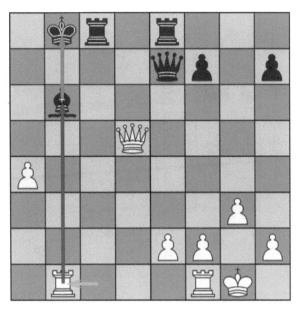

24. A pin occurs when a piece is attacking another piece and the piece in between can't be moved. Source: I, Alex valavanis, CC BY-SA 3.0 <http://creativecommons.org/licenses/by-sa/3.0/>, via Wikimedia Commons: https://commons.wikimedia.org/wiki/File:Chess_pin_rook.png

3. Skewer

A skewer is similar to a fork but involves a line of attack rather than diagonal or orthogonal lines. In a skewer, a piece attacks another piece that is in line with a more valuable piece behind it. For example, a rook skewers a pawn and a queen behind it.

Skewers force the opponent to either sacrifice the front piece to save the more valuable piece behind or move the threatened piece and lose the momentum. Like forks, skewers gain material by bringing multiple enemy pieces under threat simultaneously.

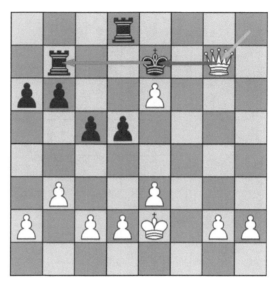

25. Skewers are similar to forks but involve a line of attack. Source: I, Alex valavanis, CC BY-SA 3.0 <http://creativecommons.org/licenses/by-sa/3.0/>, via Wikimedia Commons: https://commons.wikimedia.org/wiki/File:Chess_skewer_queen.png

Forks, pins, and skewers are three key tactics that involve multiple threatened enemy pieces. Mastering these attacking tactics and looking for opportunities to utilize them will improve your attacking play in chess.

Laws of Defense

1. **Detect and Counter Your Opponent's Plan or Threat:** To defend effectively, you must first understand what your opponent is trying to achieve with their moves. Analyze their strategy and calculate any possible threats. Then determine the best way to counter their plan and disrupt their attack.

---

2. **Make Your Opponent's Attacking Pieces Inactive**: Move your pieces to block or restrict the mobility of your opponent's attacking pieces. Do not allow strong attackers like bishops and queens to operate freely. Try to trade off overly aggressive pieces if possible.

3. **Do Not Move Your Pawns When You Are Under Attack:** Moving pawns when defending usually weakens your position. Only move pawns if there is a tactical reason to do so. Otherwise, try to keep them as stationary shields.

4. **Identify and Strengthen Your Position's Weaknesses**: Look for any weaknesses or vulnerabilities in your formation that your opponent could potentially exploit. Try to shore up these weaknesses by bringing over defending pieces or trading off ill-placed pawns.

5. **Protect and Keep Your King Safe:** Your top defensive priority should always be the safety and protection of your king. Make sure that your king has shelter from enemy attacks and is well guarded by other pieces.

6. **Do Not Be Passive in Your Defense**: A purely passive defense usually leads to a worse position over time. Look for tactical opportunities to counterattack, trade pieces, and disrupt your opponent's plans while defending. An active defense is usually better than a passive one.

A successful defense involves calculating threats, controlling key squares, minimizing weaknesses, protecting the king, restricting enemy activity, seeking tactical opportunities, and being proactive rather than passive.

Balancing attack and defense is an art form that chess players spend a lifetime perfecting.

Key Takeaways

- Attack and defense are essential in chess to win games, gain advantages, and maintain balance. Strong attackers know how to defend well and vice versa.

- Common attacking tactics include forks, pins, and skewers that threaten multiple pieces simultaneously.

- A good defense involves calculating threats, controlling key squares, minimizing weaknesses, active king protection, restricting enemy activity, tactical counter play, and an active rather than passive approach.

- Balancing attack and defense is an important chess skill, where mastery of both sides is required to succeed. Strong players know how and when to switch between attacking and defending based on their current position and the state of the board.

Chapter 6: Phases in the Game of Chess

The strategies you use in chess mainly depend on your knowledge of the phases of a game. In this chapter, you will learn about each phase in detail.

The Opening

The opening is an important part of the game that sets up the rest of the game. You need to have a good opening to do well in both the middlegame and endgame.

The opening phase lasts for about 10 to 20 moves. It is where you develop and control the center of the board, deploy your pieces, and gain space. A well-planned opening gives you more active pieces and better positions for your other pieces.

As a beginner, you should mainly focus on basic opening principles like controlling the center, developing pieces, and gaining space. Memorizing long opening lines is not necessary at your level.

However, some memorization can still be useful. You can memorize the first 3 to 5 moves of the most common openings to have some basic strategic understanding and specific plans from the very first move. This becomes more useful as your skills improve.

As you progress to intermediate levels, you will need to start memorizing more complex opening variations and lines up to 10 to 15 moves in. Being familiar with common tactical themes in various openings helps you play strategically in the middle game.

Only experienced players need to have in-depth memory of specific opening lines going 20 moves or more. But even for them, understanding opening principles and plans is more important than just blindly following memorized variations.

26. *Example of a basic chess opening. Source:*
https://getmega.ghost.io/content/images/2022/01/7-3.jpg

Objectives of the Opening Phase

Developing Pieces: This means bringing out your minor pieces (bishops and knights) and deploying the queen to an active position early in the game. Developing pieces allows you to gain control of the center and create attacking chances in the middle game.

As a beginner, your primary focus should be simply bringing out all your pieces as soon as possible, preferably by move 10. As you improve, you can learn to develop pieces strategically to specific squares for maximum impact.

Controlling the Center: You want to control the center squares (d4, e4, d5, and e5) with your pawns and pieces to restrict your opponent's pieces and gain more influence over the board.

In the opening, focus on controlling the center with pawn moves like e4, e5, d4, or d5. Later, reinforce the center with pieces like knights, bishops, and the queen. Controlling the center in the opening gives you big advantages in the middle game.

Sheltering the King (Castling): Castling quickly (moving the king to the kingside or queenside castle) shelters your king and places the rook into an active position to participate in the attack.

For beginners and children, the goal should simply be castling as soon as possible, usually within the first 10 moves. With experience, you'll learn to delay castling to unsettle your opponent's plans.

The Middle Game

The middlegame refers to the phase of the chess game after the opening but before the endgame. It is characterized by more complex tactical opportunities as pieces are developed and deployed on the board.

Key Characteristics:

- Pieces are developed and positioned, but most of them remain on the board
- Control of the center is still contested
- Tactical threats and combinations become more important
- Both sides aim to improve the positioning of their pieces

The transition from the opening to the middlegame typically happens when:

- Central pawns have been played (e.g., pawns on e4, d4, e5, d5)
- Both sides have developed most of their minor pieces (knights and bishops)
- Queens are involved in the game
- Some pieces have been eliminated

However, the middlegame phase cannot be precisely defined, and there is no fixed number of moves that marks this transition. It is a gradual process as more pieces are developed, and the initial strategic plans of the opening give way to greater tactical opportunities in the middle game. Strategic objectives also shift from center control to play on the kingside, queenside, or both wings.

27. Example of middlegame phase. Source:
https://images.chesscomfiles.com/uploads/v1/images_users/tiny_
mce/NathanielGreen/phpMrXF50.png

Key Activities in the MiddleGame

1. Coordinating Pieces

One of the main objectives in the middlegame is to coordinate the movements of your pieces to maximize their impact. This means bringing them to squares where they:

- Support each other either offensively or defensively

- Place pressure on the opponent's weaknesses

- Defend threats while retaining mobility

To achieve coordination, pieces often need to be transferred from one wing to another. Knights, in particular, excel at hopping around the board to reach optimal outposts.

Coordination of rooks also becomes more important as open files and diagonals start appearing.

Proper coordination of pieces allows you to launch attacks with combined threats, meet the opponent's attacks with double or multiple defenses, and constrict the opponent's pieces by targeting important squares they want to occupy.

2. Attacking Opponent's Fortifications

As soon as central pawn structures stabilize, players seek to undermine the opponent's control of key squares, diagonals, and open files. By targeting opponent's fortifications with tactics and combinations:

- Outposts on the board occupied by opponent's pieces can be challenged
- Threats can be made along uncovered diagonals or open files
- Isolated, backward, or doubled pawns become targets
- Pieces defending the opponent's king become overloaded

The types of fortifications commonly attacked are outposts, diagonals occupied by bishops, defended pawn chains, open files for rooks, and pieces defending the opponent's king.

Complex tactical motifs often arise when attacking an opponent's structural strengths - from forks, pins, and skewers to more advanced tactics.

3. Formulating Strategic Plans

While the opening aims to develop pieces and control the center, the middle game is when concrete strategic plans start coming together. Players formulate plans to attack:

- King by targeting kingside pawns

- Queen's wing by overloading defenses on that flank

- Both wings simultaneously

Other common strategic plans:

- Isolating and targeting the opponent's unopposed bishop

- Breaking down the opponent's pawn structure from the flanks

- Launching a minority attack against the opponent's isolated queen's pawn

As the game continues, players often abandon initial plans that fail and formulate new strategic ideas based on the evolving position. The ability to formulate, adjust, and carry out concrete strategic plans is a key marker of chess mastery in the middlegame phase.

The Endgame

The endgame refers to the final stage of a chess game where most of the pieces have been traded, and only a few remain, typically kings, a few minor pieces, and pawns. It is characterized by:

- Simpler strategic possibilities

- More precise and calculating play

- Gradual advancement of remaining pawns

- Direct attack of the opponent's king

Endgames require different skills compared to the middlegame. Positional and strategic nuances become less important while tactics diminish. Instead, players must calculate variations with precision and accurately evaluate minimal material advantages.

28. Chess endgame example. Source:
*https://images.chesscomfiles.com/uploads/v1/images_users/tiny_*
mce/ColinStapczynski/php9mwM2j.png

Distinctions between the Middlegame and Endgame

The middlegame and endgame differ in the following ways:

- **Piece Activity:** In the middlegame, most pieces are active and tactical opportunities abound. Only a few pieces remain in the endgame, and their activity is more limited.

- **Strategic Possibilities:** The middlegame has many strategic possibilities with attacks on both wings. The endgame has fewer strategic choices and more gradual maneuvering of pawns and remaining pieces.

- **Complexity**: The middle game features more complex tactical motifs and calculations. The endgame is less complex and relies more on precise, basic calculations.

- **King Activity:** For safety, the king is mostly passive in the middlegame. In the endgame, the king often becomes an active piece, supporting pawns and attacking the opponent's king.

- **Material:** Most pieces remain on the board in the middle game. Few remain in the endgame, typically a few pawns and one or two minor pieces, along with both kings.

Main Themes in the Endgame

1. Promotion of a Pawn

One of the primary objectives in the endgame is promoting a pawn to a queen to get a checkmate or gain an attacking advantage. There are several strategies to facilitate pawn promotion:

- **Clearing Obstacles:** Players move their pieces to clear a path for the pawn's advance by capturing or threatening enemy pieces that could block it.

- **Overprotection:** Other pieces are often used to defend or cover the advance of the pawn, protecting it from capture.

- **Preventing Blockade:** Players seek to prevent enemy pieces from blockading the advancing pawn, either by capturing or threatening those pieces.

- **Pawn Sacrifice**: In some cases, a pawn is sacrificed to create a passed pawn that cannot be blocked, making its promotion almost inevitable.

2. Activating the King

Whereas the king generally plays a defensive role in the middlegame, it often becomes an active piece in the endgame:

- **Centralization:** The king moves into the center of the board to support its pawns and control key central squares

- **Attack Opposing Pawns:** The king is used to attack the opponent's pawns, making it difficult for them to advance

- **Target the Opposing King:** In some endgames, the king becomes directly involved in checkmating the enemy king

An active king can:

- Help advance and protect own pawns
- Interfere with enemy pawn advances
- Act as an extra defender
- Deliver checkmate

Promoting pawns and activating the king are the two main strategic themes in chess endgames. Proper execution of these strategies is often the difference between victory and defeat in the endgame.

Importance of Smooth Transitions

The different phases of a chess game, the opening, middlegame, and endgame, require different strategies, tactics, and skills from the players. A smooth transition between phases, in which a player can adapt their plan according to the current demands of the position, is very important for success in chess. Ineffective transitions can hinder a player's overall strategy and greatly diminish their chances of winning the game.

The transition from the opening to the middle game is particularly crucial. Players must determine when central control has been established and pieces are developed enough to shift their focus from strategic maneuvering to more tactical play. Failure to adapt one's plan from achieving space and superior development to exploiting concrete tactical opportunities can waste the benefits gained in the opening.

Similarly, the transition into the endgame requires identifying when enough pieces have been traded to justify changing strategies from complex tactical motifs to precise calculation and utilization of minimal material advantages. Players who continue middlegame-thinking in an endgame with few pieces often miss crucial possibilities that are key to winning with a pawn or piece advantage.

Overall strategy and chances of winning a chess game depend greatly on a player's ability to recognize when one phase is ending and adjust their mental approach, objectives, and methods accordingly. Smooth transitions allow a player to build on previous gains and carry advantages through different stages of the game. Ineffective transitions often mean squandering early benefits and failing to take maximum advantage of a position's possibilities in the current phase. The hallmark of chess mastery is the ability to effectively transition between phases while maintaining a coherent overall game plan.

Examples of Successful Phase Transitions

Here are some examples of successful phase transitions in chess:

Opening to Middle Game

1. Bobby Fischer's king's pawn opening against Donald Byrne in the "Game of the Century." Fischer's maneuvering in the Ruy Lopez opening allowed him to achieve a strong central position with well-developed pieces. He then skillfully transitioned into the middlegame by spotting tactical opportunities to gain material and attack Byrne's king.

2. Jose Raul Capablanca's queen's pawn opening against Siegbert Tarrasch in 1912. Capablanca achieved a solid pawn structure in the opening but refrained from exchanging pieces, preserving tension. He then skillfully transitioned into the middlegame by advancing his central pawns, undermining Tarrasch's king cover, and launching an attack that won material and, ultimately, the game.

Middlegame to Endgame:

1. Mikhail Tal's queen sacrificed against Vladimir Simagin in 1956. Tal repeatedly sacrificed material in the middlegame, undermining Simagin's king position. When the transition to endgame

occurred, Tal had just two rooks and a few pawns against Simagin's rook and knight. But Tal skillfully transitioned his attack, checking Simagin's king with one rook while advancing passed pawns with the other to achieve victory.

2. Garry Kasparov's pawn grab against Nigel Short in 1993. Kasparov sacrificed a pawn in the middlegame to create weaknesses in Short's camp. When most pieces were traded, and an endgame ensued, Kasparov skillfully transitioned his play by advancing his passed pawns, activating his king, and coordinating his remaining pieces to win the game.

These examples illustrate how world-class players can smoothly transition their strategies and tactics as the phases of the game change, exploiting the positional strengths they gained in previous stages to achieve victory.

Key Takeaways

- The opening phase typically lasts for the first 10 to 20 moves. The objectives are developing pieces, controlling the center, and castling the king. Memorizing openings becomes more important when your skill level increases.

- The middle game starts after the opening but before the endgame and is characterized by complex tactics as pieces are developed. The objectives are coordinating pieces, attacking fortifications, and formulating strategic plans.

- The endgame features fewer pieces and simpler strategic possibilities. The objectives are promoting pawns and activating the king. It requires precise calculations.

- The phases differ in piece activity, strategic possibilities, complexity, and king activity.

- Smooth transitions between phases are important. Failure to adjust plans from one phase to the next can squander early advantages.

- Examples show how masters transition successfully. Fischer exploited tactics in the middlegame after a strong opening. Tal sacrificed material in the middlegame and then coordinated his remaining pieces in the endgame.

Chapter 7: Getting Better in the Game of Chess

Like many complex skills, mastery in chess comes from continuous learning and improvement over a long time. Even the greatest chess masters strive to constantly sharpen and refine their game. The reason continuous improvement is so important in chess is that:

1. **The Game Is Extremely Complex:** There are an astronomical number of possible positions in chess, far more than a player can fully grasp at any level. Even grandmasters discover new ideas and insights as they study the game.

2. **Players at the Highest Level Are Constantly Improving:** To remain competitive, players must work to improve faster than their peers. Standing still often means falling behind against rapidly advancing competition.

3. **Small Refinements Make a Big Difference:** Even tiny improvements in strategic thinking, tactical vision, or positional understanding can significantly boost a player's performance.

As a result, players at all levels should aim for steady, consistent progress rather than hoping to "level up" in large jumps. Focusing on a few key areas and making them stronger with practice leads to the compound growth that marks the transition from novice to expert.

Participating in Chess Tournaments

29. You can join a chess tournament if you make enough progress.
Source:
https://unsplash.com/photos/WtdIwprWnB4?utm_source=unsplash&utm_medium=referral&utm_content=creditShareLink

Chess tournaments are held all over the world at various skill levels and formats. From small local clubs to international events like the Chess Olympiad:

- **Club/Scholastic Tournaments:** Often held regularly by chess clubs and scholastic organizations. Beginner to advanced levels.

- **Regional/National Tournaments:** Larger events that draw participants from a region or country. Separate sections for different rating levels.

- **World Championships:** Prestigious tournaments that determine the world champion in the open, women's, and junior categories.

- **International Competitions:** Events like the Chess Olympiad and Continental Championships feature teams from different nations competing against each other.

Formats vary from quick time controls to several days of play. Some tournaments use Swiss systems with multiple rounds of pairwise matchups, while others use a knockout system. Cash prizes are common for professional tournaments.

Benefits of Participating in Tournaments

1. **Meeting Other Chess Enthusiasts**: Tournaments connect players with a broader chess community. You'll meet like-minded players of various strengths with whom you can share tips, learn new ideas, and perhaps even form longer-term friendships. Regular events at your club can become a social highlight.

2. **Gaining Experience and Exposure**: Playing against a variety of opponents in a competitive setting gives you valuable practical experience that supplements study and practice. You'll be exposed to new styles of play and surprising moves that expand your vision of the game.

3. **Improving Chess Skills Through Competitive Play:** Tournament games against live opponents provide the best test of your ability and help highlight weaknesses in your play. Losses

are learning opportunities to analyze what went wrong and determine specific areas for improvement. Over time, your rating and performance will naturally rise with increasing experience.

Participating in chess tournaments offers social and educational benefits that supplement individual study. The competition and variety of opponents push your game to a higher level by exposing weaknesses and stimulating growth. Regular participation at your appropriate rating level is ideal for continuous improvement in your chess.

Joining Chess Clubs

The easiest way to find chess clubs is to search online for "chess club + your city." Most metropolitan areas have several options for different age groups and skill levels. Clubs typically meet regularly (weekly or bi-weekly) and charge a small membership fee.

To join a club, simply show up for a scheduled meeting and provide your basic info. Many clubs have an introductory period before requiring full membership. Clubs can be a great place to find regular chess partners and tournament opportunities.

Initiating a Chess Club in Your School or Community

If no suitable clubs exist locally, you can start your own! Reach out to potential members such as:

- Schoolmates or neighbors

- Local chess enthusiasts via social media

- Your school administration for support

Start small by arranging a first meeting and go from there. Many resources exist online to help form a club, including guides from the US Chess Federation.

Advantages of Chess Clubs

1. **Regular Practice and Gameplay Opportunities**: Chess clubs provide the most structured environment for playing serious games on a schedule. This consistency is invaluable for improving your chess through repeated practice.

2. **Learning from Experienced Players**: More advanced club members can offer advice, analyze your games, suggest reading material, and answer questions to speed up your growth.

3. **Creating a Supportive Chess Community:** The social bonds formed among regular club attendees create a community that motivates members to improve. Players can spur each other on through both victory and defeat, creating a healthy competitive spirit.

Chess clubs offer important benefits that individual study cannot match. Whether you join an existing club or start your own, the regular opportunities to play, learn and socialize with like-minded people in a focused environment can take your chess game to the next level. So, seek out suitable clubs in your area and consider starting one yourself if none exists!

Exploring Online Chess Platforms

Many websites offer online chess games and tools to help players of all levels improve. Popular platforms include:

- **Chess.com:** Largest site with millions of players, lessons, analysis tools, live chess, tournaments, and a rating system. There are both free and paid versions.

- **Lichess**: Free and open-source alternative to Chess.com. It also has players, lessons, analysis, live chess, tournaments, and a rating system.

- **ICC:** Internet Chess Club, a veteran platform with top grandmasters, live commentary, and assistance features. A subscription is required.

- **Chess24:** Live chess broadcasts, top-level tournaments, lessons, and training features. It requires a subscription.

- **Android/Apple apps:** There are countless chess apps that provide similar features and accessibility on mobile.

Benefits of Playing Chess Online

1. **Accessible Anytime and Anywhere**: The biggest advantage of online chess is convenience. You can play a quick game from your phone anytime, anywhere. There's always an opponent available at your skill level.

2. **Playing Against Opponents of Various Skill Levels**: With millions of players globally, you're guaranteed to find matches against opponents much weaker, stronger, or at similar levels to your own. A wide variety of opponents exposes you to diverse styles of play.

3. **Utilizing Online Learning Resources and Tutorials**: Many platforms contain large libraries of lessons, training exercises, tactic solvers, and video tutorials to supplement your learning. Some even offer live coaching and assistance features.

Online chess platforms provide an amazing number of players, resources, and tools to complement your over-the-board development. Whether you're looking for a quick game, in-depth lessons, or something in between, these sites offer unmatched accessibility and matchmaking abilities to improve your chess game. Browse the options, find platforms that fit your needs, and make the most of what today's technology has to offer chess players!

Utilizing Chess Books and Online Resources

Reading chess books and utilizing good online resources is essential for players looking to improve beyond a basic level. This is because:

- It exposes you to the wisdom and insights of chess masters throughout history. Their studies, analyses, and discoveries are distilled into the literature.

- Patterns, motifs, and strategies described in books are difficult to discover purely through one's own games. But studying them enables you to recognize and exploit them in future play.

- The analysis of classic games illustrates perfected chess thinking that you can model and incorporate into your own game.

- Tutorials and exercises in books and online resources systematically strengthen specific aspects of your chess, like calculation, strategy, visualization, etc.

Recommended Chess Books

Some of the classic chess books to consider are:

- "My System" - Aron Nimzowitsch
- "Learn from the Legends" - Chernev
- "Improve Your Chess Now" - Tal
- "Simple Chess" - Mikhail Tal

Strategies for Effective Learning

- Take notes and annotate key passages and ideas
- Replay classic game analyses on an actual board
- Attempt exercises and quizzes multiple times
- Discuss what you're learning with stronger players
- Apply principles and strategies to your own games
- Prefer sources that emphasize understanding over memorization

---

Key Takeaways

- Mastery in chess comes from continuous learning and improvement over a long time. Even grandmasters discover new ideas as they study the game.
- Players must improve faster than their competition to remain competitive. Small refinements make a big difference in performance over time.

- Participating in chess tournaments provides valuable experience, exposes weaknesses, and accelerates improvement. Playing against different opponents expands your vision of the game.

- Joining a chess club offers regular practice opportunities, learning from experienced players, and creating a supportive chess community to motivate improvement.

- Online chess platforms provide unmatched accessibility and resources to complement your over-the-board development. They offer diverse opponents and learning tools.

- Reading chess books and utilizing good online resources exposes you to the wisdom and insights of chess masters to strengthen specific aspects of your game and inform your strategies. Taking notes and replaying game analyses enhances learning.

Conclusion

That concludes this journey through the game of chess! In this book, you have learned how pieces move, the rules and goals of the game, key strategies, and tactics, as well as tips for improving skills. You have also learned about the different phases of the game and what is required to succeed in each one.

Chess is a complex game that one can spend a lifetime mastering. With enough practice, study, and play, skills can continue to be honed. Games can be played against friends, family, or at the local chess club. Analyze games to see where improvements can be made. Read books and watch videos on chess strategy and famous games by chess masters. There is always more to learn.

Most importantly, have fun with it! Chess teaches discipline, logical thinking, planning, and pattern recognition. But it should also be an enjoyable pastime. This game connects people across cultures and generations. Go ahead and share the love of the game with others. Who knows, it may even spark their interest in taking up this classic game.

References

Chase (Ed.), Visual information processing: Proceedings (pp. 215-281). New York: Academic Press.de Groot, A. D. (1965). Thought and choice in chess. The Hague: Mouton.

Chase, W. G., & Simon, H. A. (1973). The mind's eye in chess. In W. G.

Divinsky, N. (1990). The Batsford chess encyclopedia. London: Batsford.

Elo, A. E. (1965). Age changes in master chess performances. Journal of Gerontology, 20, 289-299.

Elo, A. E. (1986). The rating of chess players, past and present (2nd ed.).New York: Arco.

Frydman, M., & Lynn, R. (1992). The general intelligence and spatial abilities of gifted young Belgian chess players. British Journal of Psychology, 83, 233-235.

Gaige, J. (1987). Chess personalia: A biobibliography. London: McFarland.

Glickman, M. E. (1995). Chess rating systems. American Chess Journal, 3, 59-102.

Gobet, F., de Voogt, A. J., & Retschitzki, J. (2004). Moves in mind: The psychology of board games. Hove, U.K.: Psychology Press.

Graham, J. (1984). The literature of chess. Jefferson, NC: MacFarlane.

Holding, D. H. (1985). The psychology of chess skill. Hillsdale, NJ: Erlbaum.

Howard, R. W. (1995). Learning and memory: Major ideas, principles, issues, and applications. Westport, CT: Praeger.

Howard, R. W. (1999). Preliminary real-world evidence that average human intelligence really is rising. Intelligence, 27, 235-250.

Howard, R. W. (2001). Searching the real world for signs of rising population intelligence. Personality & Individual Differences, 30,1039-1058

Made in United States
Troutdale, OR
11/28/2023

15084486R00056